Tad Trifles

French Fries
&
Pirouettes

Preface
Boris Lermentov

Postscript
Tom Smucker

All the characters and events in this book are fictitious, and any resemblance to actual persons, living or dead, is purely coincidental.

ISBN
978-0615668000

Busy Plug Publishing
P. O. Box 1180
New York, NY
10276
www.busyplugpublishing.com

For Slidey and Lickety Rocket

Contents

Preface

There I was. All alone. Feeling sorry for myself.

My career as a dance impresario was over, shattered by the loss of my luminescent star; the imposing impossibility of ever again mounting a full staging of out signature production; and the subsequent, inevitable collapse of the dance company that bore my name and her memory.

As the bills, lawsuits, and—worst of all—the innuendo cascaded onto my overburdened shoulders I was forced to flee. Flee Monte Carlo, Europe, the Old World itself—everything that was familiar and comforting and precious—and gratefully accept the hospitality—with an offer of employment—from distant cousins in the New World. In Des Plaines, Illinois.

I was, of course, only too familiar with the transient itineraries of those of us devoted to the performing arts. My own biography—which I incorrectly assumed had reached its own conclusion—traced from Kiev to St. Petersburg to Moscow to Paris to Copenhagen to London to Monte Carlo.

And now . . . once more the vagabond, I could only hope that the business opportunity awaiting me in Illinois might yet intermingle the classic sensibilities of Francophone culture invigorated by the pan-slavic soul of Imperial Russia that had shaped and nurtured me with the now urgent infusion of financial acumen and economic largesse of North America.

Anonymous, penniless, beginning the next—and perhaps last—chapter in my life's journey. Monte Carlo to Des Plaines!

It was, they said, the largest, most creative fast food empire in the world. (An ongoing legal entanglement does not permit me to mention the name.) I would, they said—to quote the idiom—be "starting at the bottom," then quickly promoted as I "learned the business." A difficult yet necessary apprenticeship for someone accustomed to starting at the top.

Amidst my apprehensions there was one note of reassurance. Resonating with my ever-present sensitivity to historical context, I would be working inside the current, contemporary corporate architectural articulation yet uniquely—and I believed serendipitously—placed by fate only a short walk from the shrine like original "drive-in" location from whence the entire empire first staked its claim so many years ago.

And yet . . I was lost.

Utterly lost. The nomenclature, the relentless, unaltering pace of the work, the dreadfully dressed and groomed—or perhaps, to my untrained eye, undressed and ungroomed—line of customers, the repetition of cuisine, the informality of presentation, the haphazard display—or so I thought!—of individually packaged condiments. It was all so foreign to me. Too foreign for me.

So I did what I always do in times of stress. I took the train into the city and went to the ballet. Wrapped in one of my favorite fur trimmed overcoats— poignantly now my *only* overcoat— with a silk ascot salvaged from my better days, I spiritually wrapped and thereby rejuvenated my disoriented psyche within a cocoon of beautiful memories and their attendant anticipations.

Alas, another ongoing legal imbroglio does not permit me to mention the production I saw that evening, but I am permitted to say I was transported. Utterly transported. Returned if only briefly to the

Mariinsky (Kirov), the Bolshoi, Paris Opera, La Scala, that little church in Coventry.

Unfortunately, the spell was broken—if not shattered— by the well-informed, perceptive, but foul mouthed commentary I could not but overhear from behind me.

The aforementioned legal complications compel me to resist identifying by name the source of these blasphemous asides, but I am permitted to declare that I would not be free to write this much deserved —and as you shall shortly see, laudatory—preface if the young man sitting next to me—who I would only later learn was the author of the very book or e-book you hold in your hands at this moment—had not leaned over—sensing, remarkably, that my agitation was nearing the precipice of physical violence—and whispered, "Be careful, he has a lot of clout."

I was not familiar with the terminology or topography of Chicago politics at that time, but yet could apprehend the warning, and understood from the accumulation of a lifetime's experiences that the power of ballet inevitably attracts—in fact demands— attention from those who wield power in the less sublime, but inextricably entwined realms of governance and economics. Was not the Sun King himself the *danseur noble* in his own court presentations?

After the final curtain call I thanked the young man for his intervention, and as he judiciously elaborated on the near catastrophe we had just avoided, I discovered he was also perceptive about other aspects of my then current predicament.

So desperate had I been to return to the world of dance earlier that evening that I had incautiously failed to leave the world of fast food sufficiently behind me, and so was wearing—underneath my overcoat and ascot—the corporate tunic, identification badge, and de rigueur display pin promoting the currently discounted beverage size upgrade option from my employment.

Shamefully exposed. In the palace of ballet.

Or so I thought.

But no. The young man, exhibiting a remarkable familiarity with both the world of fast food service and the world of ballet, earnestly explained to me the happy confluence of what I thought had been my sartorial confusion.

At first I was merely grateful for what I mistook as simple graciousness; a desire to put me at my ease during a moment of potential public humiliation. But he communicated his opinions with such sincerity and personality combined with a blizzard of historical facts and personal anecdotes that I was not only convinced of his sincerity but the actual application of his observations to my own personal situation.

I believed I had reached the end when he convinced me it was possible to understand my situation as a new beginning.

Well, I ramble on, and delay your immersion in the first chapter of this remarkable book, and the moment when you learn what I learned that night. That there is a connection, a delightful connection—an important, vital, visceral connection—between ballet and fast food, between pirouettes and french fries.

One last personal note, if I may.

I now own—no make that—since our gratifyingly successful public offering—*share* ownership with the public—and manage a substantial and diversified collection of franchised food outlets—from kiosks to upscale casual—and anticipate parlaying and utilizing the skills, relationships, and real estate thusly developed to replicate, yet update, in this remarkably fertile location, the network of dance—and now dance/exercise—studios I once—briefly, so many, many years ago—established in the United Kingdom and Normandy.

And, dare I say it, as you may infer if you read through the unfolding chapters, I may even return to that role once so thoroughly familiar and then nearly discarded and forgotten—shaping, enabling, creating—behind the stage and screen.

None of it would have happened had I not sat next to Tad Trifles in my Old World coat over my New World tunic that night of classical ballet in front of the future mayor of Chicago.

> BORIS LERMENTOV
> *Founder and CEO*
> *Ivan the Edible*™
> *Giselle's Delis*™
> *Little Red Shoes Studios*™

1

Lost In Paris

And there I was. All alone. Feeling sorry for myself.

Why wasn't I happy? I had achieved my lifelong ambition: studying ballet on a so-called genius grant at the Paris Opera. (OK, it wasn't strictly speaking a genius grant, but it was a scholarship of sorts; actually, as I discovered, really not enough to live on in Paris without finding *some way* to obtain some extra money.)

But I had solved that problem (the money, don't ask) and was sitting in an American hamburger chain (which I can't mention by name, and *no doubt* you know why if you have even looked at the internet once in the last year), feeling miserable.

I *loved* the Paris Opera, the classes, the students, the river, the history, the museums, the wine, the coffee, the cafes, the cheese. But the truth was . . . I was *homesick.* So I did what I always do in times of stress. I went out for a burger and fries. And a shake. (OK, maybe it was a frappe or an ice cream based desert beverage with a trademarked name that I'm not going to mention, but it was *similar* to a milk shake.)

And that, of course, *instantly* made me feel better, until I started to digest my meal (physically and emotionally) and started feeling worse.

What was I doing? Why was I jeopardizing my position at the most coveted barre in the world? Why was I returning to that only too familiar cul de sac of self-loathing and physical violence that always ended in interpersonal and litigious trouble in the past? I might as well, I thought, just call it quits and grab the next flight home. After I finished my french fries.

Then I saw her.

Call her Marie, Maria, Matilda, Madeleine, Margot, Moira, Natalie, Ninette, Nora, Tatiana, Tamara, Carlotta, Agrippina, Galina, Vanessa, Diana, or Suzanne. She was all of them and more to me. Still merely a student, but soon, we all assumed, (correctly, as it turned out, if you count ballet *and* figure skating continental television contests and her astounding ubiquity in chanson videos) to be the brightest star in the greatest constellation in the firmament of dance.

And here she was. Her every movement a testament to her training, innate athleticism, and nobility of execution. Even in that regrettably unidentifiable fast food emporium in Paris. Her entrance the beginning of an enchainement that combined a muted but distinct assemble of a ports de bras, glissade, and pirouette en dehors that concluded with the purchase . . .of an order of french fries!

I was enchanted, and yet confused, both horrified and thrilled. How could someone with such grace, such poise, such stamina and power intend to eat the same deep fried potatoes I could not resist myself yet felt had doomed my chances for success in the only world I thought I cared about?

Somehow, something deep inside (the both of us) compelled me to stand up, walk over (or rather, glide as if pulled forward by an overwhelming power) and introduce myself. And . . . she said hello, she recognized me!

We talked. We ate. We shared her special sauce. (more on that later.) And then we walked along the boulevards. We laughed, we cried, we talked some more. We ordered more french fries.

And when that marvelous, enchanted day was over, that day I learned so much, we went our separate ways.

Because I knew now what I had to do.

Like so many expatriates before me, Paris, the ballet, and a ballerina had forever altered my existence, had revealed a new universe and my place in it. And that knowledge compelled me to return. Back to my native land and its cuisine. To write this book.

Of course, I remained to finish out my course work under the terms of my scholarship. And not, as some have implied lately in the tabloid press, (and their cousins on that awful locally syndicated show that intrudes each night right after the network news, at least in the Midwest), because certain legal issues were at that time unresolved back in the States.

No, I remained to absorb everything I could. Of course I was relieved when that whole painful ordeal was settled out of court and the way was cleared for my return to reclaim my position as spokesperson for Prince Hamburgers.

And I was confident that when it would be time to officially bid adieu to Paris I would have mastered my technique and interpretive powers to take advantage, as it were, of my small stature and so continue starring as an adolescent, if not completely juvenile danseur, in those signature roles which had endeared me to audiences across the heartland of the USA, especially south central Ohio, especially at Christmas time.

But most of all, I was eager to work out my revolutionary combination diet and exercise regime that fused fast food and ballet

And it was all because of her.

Questions have been raised, unfairly, about why she remains anonymous, some insinuating that I am only interested in maintaining complete control over the royalties from my books and DVDs and streaming videos. Completely false!

She remains anonymous because that's what she prefers. If you know *anything* about the world of contemporary ballet inspired music videos her identity is obvious. Yet when we went our separate ways that magic and mysterious evening it was because we both had reached an unshakably profound belief in and understanding of each others separate destinies.

She knew that she would be a star if not *the star*, and I would return to deepen the connection between my dancing and my multimedia advocacy for the fast food industry, as well as other clients.

That's how we left it, that's how we wanted it, and that's how it will remain.

Now, let me describe what I discovered.

2

French Fries

Baked, boiled, grilled, fried, poached, roasted, or sauteed. What's the secret of French cooking?

Bechamel, beurre, bordelaise, or pistou. The sauce!

That's what I discovered.

It's the sauce.

But first.

The sauce on what?

Fresh cooked and consistent.

Make no mistake. Whatever and wherever you may order, do not accept it if it's old and stale.

You really *must* eat fast food immediately after final preparation. That's why we call it *fast*! Do *not* eat warmed over burgers or cooked, cooled, and then warmed up fries or pre-mixed shakes. Insist on fresh thawed and fried! If it isn't fresh from the freezer it's not fast food.

And insist that it's consistent.

You should expect to patronize your favorite fast food franchise and order your favorite menu item and receive *exactly* the same presentation, packaging, aroma, taste and texture, whatever the location. Every time. Anytime. Everywhere. Anywhere.

This is the genius, THE fast food brand identity. Like ballet.

Both are executions of classic forms and gestures distilled and refined into their essence. A pirouette en dehors on pointe is a pirouette en dehors on pointe! French fries are french fries! That's what we expect and that is simply what must be demanded! Standards have to be maintained.

"But Tad," you say, "my favorite fast food chain opened so many new locations I can no longer count on the consistency and freshness I once expected whenever and wherever I might purchase french fries, for instance."

You are unfortunately correct. All too correct. And that is why I have developed THE TAD TRIFFLES FAST FOOD GOURMET REPORT AND APP.™

The spread of national and then global fast food empires has been justly greeted with relief by both world travelers like myself, and foreign locals who have yearned to not only hear and see but taste the genius of our American entrepreneurial cuisine, as illustrated by my own shared story in Chapter 1.

Now we must accept the challenge, understanding that we are the fast food national and global connoisseurs and gatekeepers.

Just as others through the centuries protected and improved ballet while it was spreading out from Italy to France and then to Russia, so we must refuse to frequent those few establishments that tarnish the reputation of the industry as a whole, and diminish our own personal fast food experiences.

A small monthly charge will give you access to an interactive website, smartphone and tablet app, and/or monthly print report, allowing you to instantly identify and certify those locations that maintain the high standards we expect and will demand, and name those locations it is prudent to avoid.

See the Appendix of this book for current availability and resolution (outside of court I might add) of the various unwarranted legal actions that have attempted to silence this effort to disseminate information with slanderous accusations.

Second.

The Sauce.

Step back for a moment. While we return to the ballet.

When we are moved by the classic choreography and music of the greatest works performed by the greatest ballerinas and greatest corps de ballet we are NOT moved by meddling with the classic structures we expect, in fact, demand. Like hot, fresh, lightly salted french fries! The parameters have been established in the tug and pull of history.

But we do expect interpretation, individuality. We know which ballerinas are universally admired, and among them, which are personal favorites, or which ones move and delight us with their individuality.

That's the sauce! The interpretation.

So. You have successfully ordered and received the fast food that meets or exceeds your expectations. Now you must select and then apply the appropriate sauce. For you. Appropriate for you. As I was taught that special afternoon in Paris.

"But, Tad," you say, "we're just talking about some darn french fries."

Exactly!

What is the traditional sauce for french fries?

There are national preferences. Just like in ballet. In the British Isles and parts of Canada the sauce of choice is often malt vinegar. In much of France and Belgium it would be mayonnaise. But here in the good old USA, it is tomato ketchup.

Yes, tomato ketchup!

Have you ever really thought about ketchup? And I mean focused, concentrated, meditated. I have.

It's not all the same. If the financing comes through, and I am confident it will, you will soon be able to order my TAD TRIFLES KETCHUP SAMPLER™ and finally discover *which ketchup,* from SUPER TANGY™ to CLASSIC HEARTLAND™ to NOVELLE FRANCAIS™ (and at least three more from our laboratories) is the one that fits your ketchup profile and will satisfy your ketchup cravings.

Then you will understand, as I did that extraordinary afternoon in Paris, (as she dipped that small deep fried potato in the specially prepared ketchup she carried with her and chewed it in that impossibly small mouth and swallowed it down that impossibly long neck) that when you have fresh french fries with individually matched ketchup you will finally feel the full fast food experience. An experience you felt and knew must exist somewhere but had somehow eluded you and now you will know why.

And what about the mayonnaise? Is it wrong to prefer mayonnaise if one, for instance, developed a preference for all things Benelux during time in Brussels? Of course not.

If all proceeds as it should marketing our ketchup, and I am confident it will, we next roll out TAD TRIFLES MAYONNAISE MEDLEY™ once we settle on our palette selection. Aioli, Andalouse, Americaine, Bicky, Pickles? (Sorry no poutine, that's not a sauce.) If you would like to contribute, please access the website mentioned in the Appendix and click on SHARE YOUR MEMORIES OF MAYONNAISE.

"But Tad," you say, "What if I just walk or drive in for some fries as an impulse purchase and don't have my TAD TRIFLES KETCHUP SAMPLER™ with me?"

Good question. Unfortunately, there are regional variations in the condiments offered by most (but not all) nationwide fast food chains. Shocking but true. And that is why if you subscribe, THE TAD TRIFFLES FAST FOOD GOURMET REPORT™ will periodically mail you an invaluable laminated wallet-sized CONDIMENT ALERT™ update or tablet and smartphone app that you can't afford to miss.

Again, see the Appendix for details.

OK, that's the sauces.

So. You have purchased your fast food and received the menu item you are accustomed to and deserve. And you have selected or brought with you exactly the sauce you find pairs best with your order.

You eat. You expect to be both reassured and transported. And you have been and you are.

Now, before that evaporates, before you are returned to the drab formless misery of day to day existence that we try to ignore yet see all around us, before your body forgets its gratitude for the sublime snack you just shared, get to the barre. Get to the barre! And practice. Practice! Improve. Refine!

"But, Tad," you say, "I don't live near a dance studio or have the time or money to travel to Paris or St. Petersburg."

You don't need to. Just see the guide in The Appendix of this book to my approved dance studios. Or better yet, find the ordering information for my own soon to be released line of ballet exercise DVDs and subscription only streaming videos.

Then, using my own videos you will exercise *with me.*

You may be watching on your high-def HD TV, your tablet, cell phone, or e-reader in your home, at work, in a parking lot, or in the Men's or Women's

Room at Union Station, but you will also be in the studio, at the barre *with me*.

Together we will strengthen and refine our bodies, together we will not exercise those french fries away from us, (as if they are something *evil!*) but exercise them into us so they become our plie or pirouette, as we are fueled both physically and artistically by our fast food experience.

Will it be tiring? Yes.

Will it be boring? No.

Will it be rewarding? Yes.

Will you let your subscription lapse and not pay for a full year after the free trial period ends? No.

Will you see dramatic changes in your physical appearance, artistic temperament, social life, sex life, spirituality, political philosophy, and employment prospects? Yes.

How can I be sure?

Because in all my years dancing, singing, teaching, pitching products or appearing as a spokesperson I have NEVER enjoyed anything as much as the recording of these exercise dance videos.

Frankly, I am now convinced that this was always my destiny, the medium for which my particular gifts of expression, instruction, and intimate encouragement and communication were most suited,

Others have commented on the magic that occurs between myself and the camera when I am exercising and I concur. The knowledge that one must reach across a gap of time and space, and the realization that one has the talent and the training to do so, adds an extra, impossible to verbalize dynamic, demanding a re-evaluation of one's own career path.

I do not believe it is permissible to throw one's gifts away, regardless of how many thoughtless critiques, hostile reviews, unexpected legal proceedings, and spiteful refusals by national retail chains to carry my DVDs.

No, they have only made me more determined, more ambitious, more insistent, more assured and more aggressive. I must communicate. I will communicate. With my body and my mind.

The camera is my muse, and it will carry me. And if I have anything to say about it, we will carry you with me to a new stage of self-appreciation, health and acceptance of the world of classical ballet and classical fast food. If you could, no make that when you will, watch my videos you would, no make that you will, be forced to say, "Tad, I agree."

3

The Black Swan

Many of my friends, fans, and family have remarked over the years about my remarkable resemblance to Tyrone Power (and obviously, Douglas Fairbanks, and let's be honest, Johnny Depp, but not so much Keith Richards). So it was only natural that I would be intrigued by the possibility, when it was first suggested, of starring in a re-imagining of Mr. Power's classic 1942 Technicolor pirate swashbuckler, with Maureen O'Hara, *The Black Swan*.

As a ballet.

Which would then, I naively believed, leave the door open to a movie adaptation.

After all, fencing and ballet share roots stretching back to the royal courts of France. And what do pirates bring to mind? Hearty appetites and lots of exercise. So what would be the logical next step after my exercise ballet videos and fast food gourmet guides?

Want to look like Tyrone Power, or Douglas Fairbanks, or Johnny Depp? Or me if the movie ever gets made? Then buy my rope and swordplay exercise videos: *Slash And Sling Your Way To A New Body.* And a commemorative tie-in beverage mug or speciality sandwich or whatever, details still in negotiation (with a *major* fast food franchise).

That was the idea. Identify a need and meet it. A complete multi-media campaign to compliment the *Original The Black Swan Remake* ballet and movie.

Of course, anyone who worships at the shrine of culture knows *Swan Lake.* I've danced *Swan Lake.* (OK, maybe not professionally, but I worked for weeks in the box office of a legitimate commercial presentation.)

But no, I was not aware, when we were first shopping our proposal, that there was a different production in the works without the *The* titled *Black Swan,* NOT about pirates, and more or less about *Swan Lake* with a rather negative attitude towards mothers, exercise, and ballet itself.

And no, I was not aware that a stock photo of a ballerina that we used in our prospectus resembled

Natalie Portman. Who doesn't resemble Natalie Portman?

OK, it's true, I do not approve of analyzing and dramatizing the disturbed and disturbing inner life of some ballerinas and for that matter, movie stars, or their mothers. That's on the record.

I only "went off" in the interview clip everyone insists on watching on the internet, to establish for the public record that my *Original The Black Swan Remake* would be a tasteful homage signalling a return to the energetic high jinx, wholesome romance, aggressive expansionist economics, national greatness, and military intervention of an earlier era.

Which is no doubt why it has been ignored or worse suppressed and slandered because the mainstream media prefers to promote its own twisted, dispiriting view of human nature, and I might add, twisted view of the world of ballet in toto.

Sure, blame the mother. Well, I for one do not blame the mother. I learned a lot entering the Little Mister Hamburger contests as a kid. Of course, I was too young to understand that multiple entries under multiple names were not only frowned upon but forbidden. No, I didn't have polio. But was it such a stretch when in fact I was performing without having totally recovered from the chicken pox?

It's true. I did use the so-called "unhappy childhood" defense in that so-called assault case, but tell me exactly what you would have done differently if you were facing jail time again? My lawyers said it was the only option, and here I am today. Case closed, as they used to say on the set of that police procedural I was cast in with a reoccurring part when it was canceled.

I am not a political person, but I wonder about the agenda of those who label the *1942* (emphasis added) *The Black Swan* as sexist, racist, and what have you. Are they serious?

Come on! We are talking about Tyrone Power and Maureen O'Hara! George Sanders and Anthony Quinn! With a score by Alfred Newman! Adapted from the novel by Rafael Sabatini! Screenplay by Seton I. Miller and Ben Hecht! Directed by Henry King! Produced by Robert Bassler! Cinematography by Leon Shamrey!

Yes, it does take place in Jamaica, and there is only one black character. But that is because the dramatic emphasis, brilliantly articulated in the movie by Tyrone Power and by myself in our proposed adaptation, highlights that moment in history when the English pirates prove that underneath it all they always wanted to be loyal members of the Empire and were ready to "join the establishment" as soon as the good king replaced the bad king and gave them amnesty. Or at least some of them. The good ones. Led by Tyrone Power. And now me.

And that is why Tyrone Power/me has to go undercover as a pretend bad pirate to protect Maureen O'Hara/uncast (*of course* we'd love to have Jennifer Lawrence or Kristen Stewart, and once again I was quoted out of context) from the real bad pirates.

Because there are still bad pirates. As well as sneaky, crooked politicians who pretend to be good like Maureen O'Hara's boyfriend in the movie. And good pirates that sometimes have to pretend they are still bad pirates. Even or especially today.

And so that is why the good pirates reappear in our update in the by now "controversial" dream sequence flash forward coda in those wall street style white shirts and power ties and big suspenders.

After the drama and anxiety of 2008 who was not inspired by the amazing recovery of many of our major (and minor) financial institutions even though they were forced to take a government bailout whether they wanted one or not?

And the patriotism of all those physics students who did not abandon Wall St. and return to their studies, but kept inventing new financial products too complicated for the rest of us to understand?

Or those courageous politicians who refused to vote for more Big Government regulations no matter how often they were attacked by the elite media commentators?

You built the wealth of our new empire, good pirates of the new millennium! Now join all the other good pirates who are working sometimes very far from company headquarters to build more wealth, this time legally! Especially if and when the Supreme Court throws out those regulatory agencies that can only discourage people from wanting to get rich and create new jobs.

And no, I was not aware there was another *The Black Swan*, a book with a peculiar, yet lucrative, look at stock picking and market timing and portfolio balancing and Plato and the Nobel Prize in economics and who knows what else, set in imaginary lands named Mediocristan and Extremistan.

But I say even to fans and followers of that *The Black Swan*, and any other oddball best sellers, come join us as well. Add your offbeat ideas, complaints, impulse purchases, and weird theories to the mix.

And I even say also to those Monday morning quarterbacks, as irritating as they may be, sure now you say you knew all along that sub-prime mortgages were dangerous, who is going to believe that? But now it's time to get positive! And remember to exercise, so check out my videos.

The era of privateers is drawing to a close. The war with Spain or whoever is over. We won! Or are getting close. Help us celebrate. That's the uplifting message we want to leave the audience with. And not just about the past.

That leaves us to one final ugly, unfortunate slander from the lamestream media that placed the cart of financing before the horse of my convictions.

No, I was not obligated in any way by the underwriting I had obtained to include the, as it's now commonly referred to, "hedge fund coda" or even the "pirates eat a fish sandwich" dance sequence. Don't pirates eat fish?

I did not alter the production to suit the whims of my financial backers, as claimed. I sought out financial backing from those fast food and financial products franchises, SuperPacs, think tanks, venture capitalists, and pension fund managers who I believed would underline the underlying message of our *Original The Black Swan Remake.*

Namely, that there is a time and place for privateers and outlaws, and so let's admit it and celebrate all that rowdy fun and stuff stolen from our enemies. And then there's a time and place to pledge allegiance to your country and defeat for those who won't.

I was merely trying to dramatize through dance and cinema the similarities between when Bette Davis was Queen and the conflicts of today, along with some timeless but up to date advice on what to eat and how to stay in shape. And a few investment options.

If that makes me too relevant or too popular or "surprisingly successful at finding investors for what some would consider his long shot Broadway and Hollywood productions" as one of the trade papers put it, then I plead guilty. And not for the first time.

4

The Welterweight

It started with the simplest of ideas.

One that occurred to me during one of my unfortunate incarcerations.

Boxers and wrestlers are like dancers.

They train.

They practice.

They perform for the public. Often in a lot of pain from injuries

So why not a ballet about a boxer, or maybe a wrestler? Or a movie about a boxer or wrestler who is also a ballet star? And has some pirates in it?

How about one of those inspiring movies about a boxer who is also a dancer who never got the breaks he deserves and has a son with an injury or a wife or loyal dog, and he's patriotic, and wins the big fight in the next to last scene?

And . . . let's face it, at the moment the public is suspicious of athletes (or politicians) with big, bulky muscles. Maybe that means they're on steroids! So why cast for a *heavyweight* boxer? It can be just as inspiring with a boxer in the welterweight division, or even lighter.

You don't have to be *gigantic* to win in the next to last scene or even be emotional in a tragic sort of way by losing but maintaining your dignity or even dying in a real tear jerker if the investors want to go that route.

Obviously, we would be sincerely thrilled to get Mickey Rourke or Nicholas Cage or Angelina Jolie or Jennifer Lawrence cast as the lead. But if none of them work out, I'd take it, which actually, when you think about it could even work out better, because of the opportunity to use someone who already knows and understands ballet and could incorporate some of those popular Asian fighting styles that favor a slimmer profile.

And so what if it has become public knowledge that I'm financing with some extra corporate tie-ins and a little product placement? I'm proud of my track record using product placement to advance the plot.

For instance. Let's say I'm training using (guess what?) my own training videos. I'm getting in shape eating at, (guess where?) my favorite fast food franchise (details still in negotiation) using my (guess what?) favorite TAD TRIFLES KETCHUP™.

How can *that* be "selling out" if I'm doing what I love and it *works*? I'm merely offering to combine and utilize the different facets of my multifaceted career. If you have to give it a name then let's call it "selling in." I'm accessing my emotional connection to *my* ketchup, *my* french fries, *my* pas de chat, *my* favorite financial products.

OK, back to the movie.

The current welterweight champion has and wastes a lot of money and he and his managers hang out with all those big shot politicians who like to waste a lot of money. Our tax money. And they are driving up the national debt but don't care, much to the disgust of myself and all the regular guys I hang out with at my dance studio in the strip mall near where I grew up.

And there's this good politician who isn't really even a politician but a clean cut financial guy and he's willing to run for office because he knows we need to reduce the national debt without driving up taxes. And has the backing of these guys who run a successful financial products franchise who are worried about the national debt.

But they know he can't win the next big election as long as everyone sees the current welterweight champ (who is also flashy and brags too much) hanging out with the politicians who don't care if they drive up the national debt.

Then the champ's backers decide that he should fight me, because I don't stand a chance and I believe in a balanced budget with no new taxes, so that will draw a big crowd. But they underestimate me and the people backing me including the financial products franchise managers and the guys who hang around the mall.

Then there's the training, the romance, the humor, the minor characters. And the big fight.

My opponent was born in Kenya but doesn't want anyone to know it. But I do. He's almost like a terrorist and religious in a foreign sort of way, (but not anything in particular that might complicate world wide distribution), and wants to bankrupt the country. It's a promise he made to his father a long time ago, or maybe his grandmother the time he visited her in Kenya, depending on our budget.

The two fighters are supporting two different candidates for President who will either balance the budget and pledge no new taxes or destroy the country with even more debt. So the candidates and their supporters will either be discouraged or confident depending on the outcome.

I'm winning, then losing, then I see my wife or the kindly old economics professor with the Austrian accent who's been managing my career after he got fired from his job at the snobby college in New England because he was warning everybody about the national debt and they didn't want to listen because they believed in wasting tax money and didn't want anyone to know the college itself was deep in debt.

And I remember what it's all about. Saving the people I love from the national debt! And no new taxes!

My opponent has me on the ropes and is getting ready for the final blow and . . . I have a secret weapon. I know ballet! But he's hitting me so hard it looks like I'm forgetting.

He's pummeling me. A left! A right! I'm almost done for. He's about to land that big blow that you can tell will end it all because the movie goes into slow motion.

And then the movie goes into *super* slow motion flashback while I remember my old ballet instructor who had to flee Sweden because he didn't like the nanny state and you think is so mean at first but later realize actually loves ballet and wants you to succeed while maintaining high standards.

Then I flashback to when I met my wife who was a ballerina in a wheelchair because a mugger injured her so she can't dance anymore.

And then back to when the college professor with the Austrian accent turned boxing manager got fired . . . and the slow motion ends because now I remember my *echappe saute* and dance out of my opponent's reach and the big blow doesn't even touch me!

And we fall into a clinch and I whisper in his ear, "Your father was way too angry about colonialism."

He's never seen or heard anything like that before so he's thrown off balance mentally and physically and trips and I hit him hard enough to knock him out but he only falls down on his knees because he's taken this illegal drug he gets from an illegal immigrant you see earlier in the movie.

But he's so demoralized by now he doesn't get up before the referee counts to ten and counts him out!

The crowd goes wild! I'm carried out of the arena by a bunch of famous choreographers making cameo appearances and some Austrian economists.

I go back to the old mall and receive a hero's welcome. These are people who understand the problem of too much national debt! And the effect of too many taxes on the real job creators!

I enter my old dance studio for sentimental reasons because by now it's Christmas Eve. The credits role as I reprise all of the main characters and solos in The Nutcracker, as only I can do because I have the uncanny ability to remain convincing as a juvenile OR adult character in ANY role and the camera pulls back, revealing snow falling outside the studio in the parking lot as I continue dancing on the inside.

My wife is with me, watching from the wheelchair, sitting next to the old professor who is probably thinking that at last, the federal budget will get balanced. And next door the financial services guys are putting the finishing touches on a new branch office!

The sound track will be a mix of standards like Tchaicovsky, dancercize hits and new music commissioned for the movie, just like *Saturday Night Fever.* At the moment, we are nearly certain that the title sequence could feature an inspiring hard rock anthem by a vocalist resembling Bruce Springsteen. But at the end with the credits rolling it will be inspiring more like Celine Dion.

I guess this is the place to clear up any confusion caused by looking for me using any of the popular internet search engines and seeing the nickname "The Dancing Rat" pop up. That is not in reference to Nutcracker roles associated with my career. Of course I can dance and have danced the Mouse Captain. But I am known for my interpretation of the Nutcracker (male lead) itself, which I graduated to well before those slanders were spread about me and my so-called organized crime "associates" and that alleged trouble with the Grand Jury testimony that can easily be taken out of context.

5

The Welterweight II

Could there be a sequel? Absolutely. And at the same time the third chapter of a trilogy. Here's how.

In his next movie, THE WELTERWEIGHT II: SHANZAI, our hero is fighting in the Eurozone or whatever it is called by now, because the governments over there obviously have a problem with their debts, so there's an exciting fight scene at the *beginning* of the movie, against the greatest fighter from one of those countries that believes in taking it easy and never having austerity. But we believe in austerity!

So that gets straightened out.

Then in a flashback we find out that while our hero was training for the fight, probably in Paris, he discovers that his exercise videos are being pirated in Asia, (OK, I'm realizing that this only works if I play the lead) and that's why I haven't seen any revenue stream from Asia even though I know I'm popular from my *Original The Black Swan Remake* and because fast food franchises are popping up all over, along with a growing interest in Classical Ballet. And exercise.

So after winning the fight in Paris or wherever I team up with one of those Bruce Lee type characters with a sense of humor to force the Chinese or whoever to let their currency float on the open market, while respecting international intellectual copyright protection, especially on DVDs and streaming videos.

This is important because the financial guys that backed all my title fights want to spread the advantages of their financial products to Asia but they won't until there are protections against the pirating of stuff like DVDs and streaming videos and whatever other kind of cutting edge technological breakthroughs come along that I can use to spread my discoveries about dieting and dancing exercise.

So that returns us to the good pirates/bad pirates theme, just like in my *Original The Black Swan Remake.* And now you can see the importance of the dream sequence flash forward coda.

THE WELTERWEIGHT™ (by now it's trademarked) and his Bruce Lee type friend get some of the pirates to become good pirates because they respect them for their fighting skills and remember some crazy stuff they all used to do together when they were younger that's shown in another flashback and they start selling authorized DVDs and help catch the pirates who stay bad and I go undercover as a bad pirate.

It's very dangerous but sometimes humorous since I can't speak Chinese. Or whatever the language is. Although I know that shanzhai is the local term for pirated illegal brand knock-offs. Who doesn't?

And there's this airline pilot from Chicago who everyone thinks is a good guy, but I can tell he is a little too concerned with his appearance and of course he is secretly flying all the latest DVDs in his suitcase so they can be illegally copied in China but he gets exposed towards the end.

Also, by now (after a flashback to a funeral establishes that my wife died after the first movie) I have a love interest, preferably an Asian Maureen O'Hara type, who is the daughter of a corrupt official and a stewardess from Chicago.

She thinks she is going to marry the good looking airline pilot who is secretly working for the bad pirates and is trying to make the good pirates look like bad pirates, including me, so she thinks I really am a bad pirate and not undercover while she is actually attracted to me and doesn't even know it!

But I can tell! And by now my rascally screen presence is so firmly established that the audience is reassured that at times, even though I act bad, just like Tyrone Power, I'm good all along underneath.

Finally we destroy all the pirated DVDs in the climactic battle/dance scene that ends with a huge explosion in a big warehouse that also houses a rehearsal space and disco utilized earlier in the movie for some of the ballet inspired dance sequence interludes. We escape in a speedboat, only because I pull off all these amazing *grand allegros* to avoid a series of smaller explosions that are leading up to the big explosion.

During which my love interest sees that I really am a good pirate in disguise (and on top of that a great dancer) and breaks up with the airline pilot who's going to jail anyway for smuggling (and for being an all around phony) and then the good pirates get to sell their authorized DVDs and revenue producing authorized streaming videos in Asia and the Eurozone and North and South America and other emerging markets and make a lot of money.

Free trade. With copyright protection. Everyone gets rich. Of course we have included at the end one of those sentimental yet humorous scenes with me and my Bruce Lee type sidekick and the kindly old economics professor turned fight promoter.

The professor is in surprisingly good shape because he doesn't believe in government controlled health care and has been secretly doing my exercises on his own initiative while watching my videos so we all decide to go out to eat at our favorite fast food restaurant.

Then they ask me to dance so after we order and sit down and eat I reprise one of my signature ballet solos, probably the one that saved us from the explosion. That makes this part a little more like Gene Kelly doing *Singin In The Rain.* Or maybe *Grease 2.*

As you can see, the parts are larger than the whole here when you have all three movies and their stage adaptations. Like *The Lion King* combined with when they made *Back To the Future* already knowing there would be two sequels or *The Godfather Trilogy.*

Therefore this is obviously NOT an attempt to "settle scores" with anybody and has NOTHING to do with *that* Black Swan or Rocky or Rambo, as was suggested in that horrible magazine (which I refuse to mention by name here and thereby give any kind of publicity, good or bad) profile for which I granted an interview in my apartment (OK, well it was a friend's apartment of equal or lesser value when there really wasn't time to clean up mine) because of its prestige and circulation.

After all three movies have been released it will become obvious that my *Original The Black Swan Remake* is a prequel that sets up THE WELTERWEIGHT™ for THE WELTERWEGIHT™ II: SHANZAI. Making it natural, eventually, for all three to get repackaged, in different formats for different markets, along with a bonus of my exercise videos. So that would make its resemblance to any other movie or movie series completely coincidental.

Come on! These movies and their stage adaptations won't even have one scene set in Philadelphia! Or Afghanistan!

In fact, at the moment we are scouting locations in the western suburbs of Chicago, so if anything you might possibly compare them more to the *Home Alone* series which I missed the auditions for when I was a child and out on tour.

Yes, I worked on tour as a child and so I understood from an early age how you pay the bills, including taxes designed to destroy small businesses and undemocratic big union dues, unlike some people who think they should have everything handed to them with the government going into debt for that reason.

I understand *personally* what happens when you go too far into debt, particularly if you borrow money from someone you think is a new friend you met at your favorite bar who is actually focused on becoming your silent, and then not so silent, business partner, if you know what I mean.

6

Puck

William Shakespeare, Felix Mendelsohn, George Balanchine, Mickey Rooney, Olivia De Havilland.

The artists linked forever in our memory with *A Midsummer Nights Dream* remind us that respect for tradition combined with new ideas kept this masterpiece alive down through the centuries as a play, ballet, and movie.

And will continue to resuscitate this perennial, if I have anything to do with it.

What would, I ask, be the natural next adaptation in the era of the viral video?

Is it not—for a play about four couples and their shifting physical attractions, pranks played, three weddings, and a play within a play—reality TV?

And what would, I ask, be the first great classic of reality TV, the Shakespeare of this art form?

Is it not—*The Real World?*

And so, would not a mash-up of *A Midsummer Nights Dream* and *The Real World*—featuring couples hooking up and unhooking and then hooking up again at the sexy conclusion—need to have the necessary mischief caused by that mashed-up classic hard to get along with MTV roommate guy *and* Shakespearean trickster—Puck?

Of course there are clearances and copyrights to sort through that might alter the final shape of our production. Our ability to pay any sort of royalty is severely limited. So anyone who keeps pressing the point about their so-called compensation will have to be dropped from the show. (You know who you are and can quit calling me at home.)

Nevertheless . . . let me state for the record that the original Puck appears in the original Shakespeare, and therefore is no longer under copyright or trademark.

And roommates or family members arguing with each other in front of a video camera or speaking directly at that camera, or waiting nervously, wondering if they are going to be eliminated from the show, or flirting while dancing at a club, or getting drunk sitting on the balcony of that fancy condo when the whole group goes on vacation with the sun setting on the ocean: these are all public domain dramatic elements that you cannot sue me or anyone else for using.

Shakespeare got his material from ancient Athens. Mendelsohn got his from Shakespeare. Balanchine got his from both of them. Max Eastman got his from all three.

I'm merely proposing that we combine those four, and offer my unique ability to act, dance, and feel comfortable, even inspired, talking about myself and other people in a documentary style TV drama. Then add—and this will, I believe, really secure the publicity—my well established (and unfair but I can live with it) characterization as a bad real world (not *The Real World*) roommate and impish but lovable eternally youthful presence.

And as a bonus, if there is the almost inevitable second season, you have the gold mine of my career as a ballet exercise entrepreneur and fast food diet and condiment guide and gourmet for plot development.

Reality TV has arrived as a maturing art form ready to be moved up market. And I'm just the Puck who can do it.

Of course, if our financing sees greater bottom line marketing potential in a darker drama, then what would be more natural for a story traditionally established in a forest setting than to highlight the survivalist, sometimes violent, as well as romantic dramatic tensions?

Shakespearean material is always getting restaged and filmed taking place in all kinds of different time periods. But why are they always from the past? What's wrong with the future? An ominous future?

Why not a grim fight to the death, roommate against roommate, couple against couple, in a futuristic simultaneously high and low tech world? A fast paced action movie in the woods utilizing hand-held cameras and some well placed special effects?

A Midsummer's Nightmare Games?

I can already hear the inevitable complaints about using special effects in a Shakespearean adaptation.

And I don't care. Jimmy Cagney with a donkey's head is a special effect, and that's in the original. I'm just thinking outside the box here.

Or am I?

7

Pan, Peter

By now he's at least a hundred years old and he never grows up. As the other characters back in England get old it seems like they kind of forget about him, but he doesn't forget about them. So he has those hundred years of memories stored up.

I mean, he doesn't have memory loss and he's been alive a long time. Shouldn't Peter Pan be played at this point by someone who can still look like a boy with the right make-up, someone familiar with Jerome Robbins choreography, someone who can still dance, someone who is clearly NOT a middle aged female musical theater star or a gymnast, someone comfortable with juvenile roles AND familiar with many (maybe too many) of life's ups and downs?

Someone who knows the history. Someone whose mother used to read him from Chapter Seven of *Wind In The Willows* while Pink Floyd's first album played softly in the motel room. A spoken word and musical combination of *Piper at the Gates of Dawn* performed just for him. Or so he thought.

And that is how he would fall asleep after the show when he was on tour and his mother's supposedly English boyfriend would drop by with his pipe and they would smoke and the boy would dream about the Greek god with goat feet who played the pan pipes, just like Zamfir.

It's heart-rending, almost tragic, or at least really sad when you think about it. Peter Pan is a hundred years old and he still looks like a boy, and the audience still wants him to act like a boy. And he's still fighting pirates.

But what boy has that many memories?

I'm just asking.

8

Lafitte

But back to historical pirates. And ballet. And diets.

With all the excitement over the Bicentennial of the War of 1812, I'm stunned there is no talk of a 3-D remake of the 1958 full color remake with Yul Brynner of the 1938 black and white *The Buccaneer* with Fredric March. Which people who know about these things say is a remake of Lord Byron's 1814 poem *The Corsair,* which sold ten thousand copies the first day it was released! And of course inspired *Le Coursaire* in 1856, still stunning in numerous revivals with the its famous *pas de deux.*

Almost two hundred years of box office magic!

Who can resist the story of Jean Lafitte, the privateer, who "removes" the cargos from ships sailing in the Gulf of Mexico, but leaves everyone alive, and then sells it at a discount in the bayous to the citizens of New Orleans.

And then, when the British attack the city, joins Andrew Jackson (Charlton Heston in the full color version) with his colorful privateer buddies, many of whom speak French, or at least have an accent like Charles Boyer, and the citizens of New Orleans, and those guys that look like Davy Crockett, and defeats the British guys who wear bright red uniforms (haven't they learned by now?) and march in straight lines. And that saves New Orleans and the whole United States.

Moral: people involved in selling what we might call "grey market" goods can actually be relied on to work with the government when the country is facing a threat to its survival.

I won't go into it here, because there are some differences between the black and white and full color versions, mainly to make room for the sultry Claire Bloom character, but in both versions, Fredric March and Yul Brynner have to put out to sea at the end, with no country to call their own, even though they saved the USA from defeat at the Battle of New Orleans!

That's historically correct, because Jean Lafitte did have to leave the USA and go back to privateering, Claire Bloom or no Claire Bloom, but why?

It was all he knew. After the war was over, why not find him a good position somewhere in the government using his deal making skills, or you know, in retail, or show business?

Moral: people involved in selling what we might call "grey market" goods who have cooperated with the government during an emergency deserve to be recognized for their patriotism, and not just at one fancy banquet and dance right after the big battle.

Even if it has to be "behind the scenes" so they are not bothered about every petty infraction but helped to establish themselves in a legitimate career. Otherwise they will be forced to return to whatever it is they were familiar with before they saved the country.

So if they do, don't rush to blame them but give them the same sympathy you give to Yul Brynner and Fredric March.

Anyway. A remake of The Buccaneer in 3-D could really take advantage of all that pirate swordplay and cannons and swinging on ropes and the rifles and bayonets in the battle scenes. As well as the French inspired cuisine (in my movies the pirates will not be chomping on one of those ridiculous overcooked gigantic chicken legs) and vigorous "old school" dancing in New Orleans.

But if there isn't, in the end, enough money to go 3-D, there is another darker story in all this about the survival of the fittest and ships sunk at sea with everyone on board and fighting in the bayous and the The Powers That Be turning against you when the war is over. And who is really to blame for the consequences when there is only a partial amnesty and inadequate funding for a 3-D remake?

I'm just asking.

French Fries & Pirouettes

9

Lopokovan Economics

Don't get me wrong. Just because I want to make a patriotic movie about working to enforce the laws and protect national security, that does not mean, and I cannot emphasize this enough, that I believe we should return to the era of big brother big nanny state controlled big culture.

Sure, I know that the great ballerina Lydia Lopokova was married to Mr. It's-OK-To-Expand-The-National-Debt-Forever-On-The-Road-To-Serfdom John Maynard Keynes. And I am aware that after World War II John Maynard Keynes helped revive Sadler's Wells and thereby help usher in one of if not *the* golden era of English ballet. I *have* heard of Margot Fonteyn.

But that was then.

The era of Big Government Ballet. In Great Britain. In the USSR. In the USA.

And that era is over.

Finished. Gone. Kaput. Into the dust bin of history with the Pony Express, player pianos, black and white TV and raising the minimum wage so often that you stop creating jobs.

Ballet has always moved towards power. From the French courts, to the Kremlin, to Keynesian tax and spend Great Britain, Republican In Name Only America and Socialistic Western Europe to . . . our current era, the era of getting government off our backs and the shackles off the multinational corporations!

This is now.

Walk past Lincoln Center in New York City as I have done and you will notice that the premier ballet venue there, (once named the New York State Theater), has been renamed the David H. Koch Theater in honor of the philanthropist, conservative political behind-the-scenes guy, chemical engineer, and really rich businessman who donated $100 million for its renovation.

Or follow the recent ballet appointments around the world as I do and you will notice that in St. Petersburg, Russia, fruit magnate (the so-called banana king) Vladimir Kekhman has *so far* poured more than

$40 million into the Mikhailovsky Theater and hired away Nacho Duato, Leonid Sarafanov, Ivan Vasilieve, *and* Natalia Osipova!

Adapt. Stay current.

Of course, we must honor our traditions.

And I do. But which ones?

What about the traditions of discovering what's beautiful inside of what's powerful *and* the other way around? Because, by the way, it is and always has been a two way street. For the beautiful *and* for the powerful.

Are you listening fast food industry? The banana king is listening. The chemical engineer conservative guy is listening.

Let's dance!

Appendix

Under advice from counsel we have removed the content of this section. We regret that it cannot be included for the historical record, but are convinced that the undocumented assertions and deeply flawed science contained in the detailed diet and exercise regimen are not simply misleading but potentially dangerous and quite possibly fatal if carried out as printed in the original edition.

The Publisher

Postscript

When one sets out to write a popular best seller, as I did with *An Inconvenient Amish Zombie Left Behind The Da Vinci Diet Code Truth,* phrases such as "potboiler" or "page turner" spring to mind. But after publication, as sales soared into the low double digits, I had reason to wonder if I had taken too literally the admonition to create "characters that leap off the page."

As *An Inconvenient Amish Zombie Left Behind The Da Vinci Diet Code Truth* penetrated that great living entity we call mass consciousness, reports were circulating that one of my fictional characters, Tad Trifles, had escaped the confines of my novel and written, published, and promoted a self-help book of his own.

I had, I confess, difficulty with this character during my decade long struggle to research and write an action packed narrative that would do justice to the War of 1812, the founding of swing state Ohio, the true history of Soft Rock, Paris, The Rapture, Goya, and the fast food rest stops along Interstate 75.

Tad Trifles was annoyed—from the day I started writing *An Inconvenient Amish Zombie Left Behind The Da Vinci Diet Code Truth*—that he would not be introduced until Chapter 21 and would not receive more "page space" as he called it. Oddly enough, he did not seem to mind the rather repugnant position I assigned him in the plot. That was a warning I ignored at my peril.

I was, of course, gratified that I had created such a compelling character, but more than a little irritated that he could not understand his status in *An Inconvenient Amish Zombie Left Behind The Da Vinci Diet Code Truth* as a minor and nearly extraneous embellishment.

In retrospect, I should have noted the trouble he was causing and refrained from using or even mentioning his character anywhere in the book. As two or three close friends have mentioned to me, the book is indeed stuffed full, some might say overstuffed, with plot twists and major and minor characters. Tad Trifles would not have been missed,

At first I tolerated the publication of his unstable mix of classical ballet and fried food, as it was an underground publication with only an underground reputation. Any publicity is good publicity and all that.

And then, as his book gained a wider audience, I met with my legal advisor and was cautioned that because I had indeed created Tad Trifles, I could, conceivably, be held libel for the potentially lethal misrepresentations about dieting and exercise published by Tad Trifles.

After further consultation we decided that the only safe course of action was to gain control of this publication, remove the dangerously toxic Appendix, and attach this clarifying Postscript.

Please be advised that this is the only authorized edition of *French Fries & Pirouettes,* and that myself and the officers and stockholders of Busy Plug Publishing will not be held accountable for the content of any other pirated or unauthorized additions, or the consequences physical or emotional of following the advice in the Appendix excised from this edition.

Three additional notes.

The Preface by one Boris Lermentov is an obvious forgery, as anyone with even a rudimentary knowledge of the history of musical cinema or frankly, access to any interview with Martin Scorcese would realize. Do the math.

Second. We shall permit Mr. Trifles his obsession with pirates and pirate movies, but I should warn readers that his sympathetic description of Jean Lafitte, who was an actual historical figure, is grossly inaccurate, and omits any mention of the true nature of much of the "cargo" Lafitte captured and sold. But I will leave it at that. For now.

I apologize to both those readers who have written me fondly of their reactions to *An Inconvenient Amish Zombie Left Behind The Da Vinci Diet Code Truth* and hope that this unfortunate episode will not detract from their enjoyment or future word of mouth that might lead to a future purchase or purchases, in print or e-book format. Let me reassure them that the dramatically low sales ranking brought on, no doubt, by this unprecedented notoriety, in no way complicates on-line availability of the original novel.

There will always be, I suppose, a potential danger in creating characters so vivid that they slip beyond the control of those authors who create them. But this will not deter me from telling those stories I feel inspired and therefore obligated to tell. Such are the risks that I assumed when I first decided to write and publish *An Inconvenient Amish Zombie Left Behind*

The Da Vinci Diet Code Truth, and I will not run from those risks now.

Finally, readers should be reassured that my advisors are convinced that because this book was created by a character of my own creation, I therefore have full legal, fiduciary, moral, literary, and quite possibly psychological rights and obligations in perpetuity to present or dispose of this book as I see fit. And so this is and will remain the only authorized edition.

Tad Trifles has been returned to the confines of *An Inconvenient Amish Zombie Left Behind The Da Vinci Diet Code Truth* where he belongs, and will not be making any further appearances in print unless I so authorize.

I toyed with the idea of removing Mr. Trifles altogether from a new, abridged edition of *An Inconvenient Amish Zombie Left Behind The Da Vinci Diet Code Truth.* But no!

Such spiteful action towards an object of my own invention would only compromise the original conception I had for a compelling but honest portrayal of life as it is really lived in an imaginary near future dystopia and thereby break the promise of artistic integrity to both those readers who had actually read *An Inconvenient Amish Zombie Left Behind The Da Vinci*

Diet Code Truth all the way from its surprise beginning to its startling conclusion.

And so we have the present volume with its peculiar history and *An Inconvenient Amish Zombie Left Behind The Da Vinci Diet Code Truth* untouched, word for word as originally made available to the public.

Tom Smucker
July, 2012

If You Enjoyed This Book You Might Also Enjoy:

An Inconvenient Amish Zombie Left Behind The Da Vinci Diet Code Truth
by Tom Smucker
Unabridged Edition

Fran Trotter's Canada: Neighbor To The North *OR* Marxist Menace?
foreword by Pud Hornets
afterword by Tom Smucker

A Reader's Guide To Characters, Locations & References In

Tom Smucker's *An Inconvenient Amish Zombie Left Behind The Da Vince Diet Code Truth Unabridged Edition,*
Tad Trifles' *French Fries & Pirouettes,*
and Fran Trotter's *Canada: Neighbor To The North or Marxist Menace*

Available from

Busy Plug Publishing
P.O. Box 1180
New York, NY
10276
www.busyplugpublishing.com

Coming soon . . .

. . . Poetry from Busy Plug!!

www.ingramcontent.com/pod-product-compliance
Lightning Source LLC
Chambersburg PA
CBHW020514030426
42337CB00011B/387